Foundational Theology

An Introduction to Christian Action

Edward Bevilacqua

Our Approach

.... *Matthew 11:30*

—Jesus of Nazareth

Kinship

No Kinship no justice, no kinship no peace, no kinship no equality

---

Foundational Theology

An Introduction to Christian Action

Edward Bevilacqua

Thriving Warrior Publishing Co.

1st Printing: June 2023

ISBN 978-1-312-45548-1

Thriving Warrior Publishing Co.
4021 N NV Hwy 160
Pahrump, NV 89060

www.ThrivingWarrior.me

Ordering Information:

Program discounts are available for inmates and others. For details, contact the publisher at the above listed address.

For all inquiries, please contact Thriving Warrior Publishing Co. at publisher@ThrivingWarrior.me.

Dedication

To my six children (Roxane Prima, Elisse Due, Edward III, Catherine Fyra, Lucia Femma and Sophia Asesta) and my granddaughters, Lana James and Ozzie: you inspire me to remind myself daily that, "Yesterday was the only easy day".

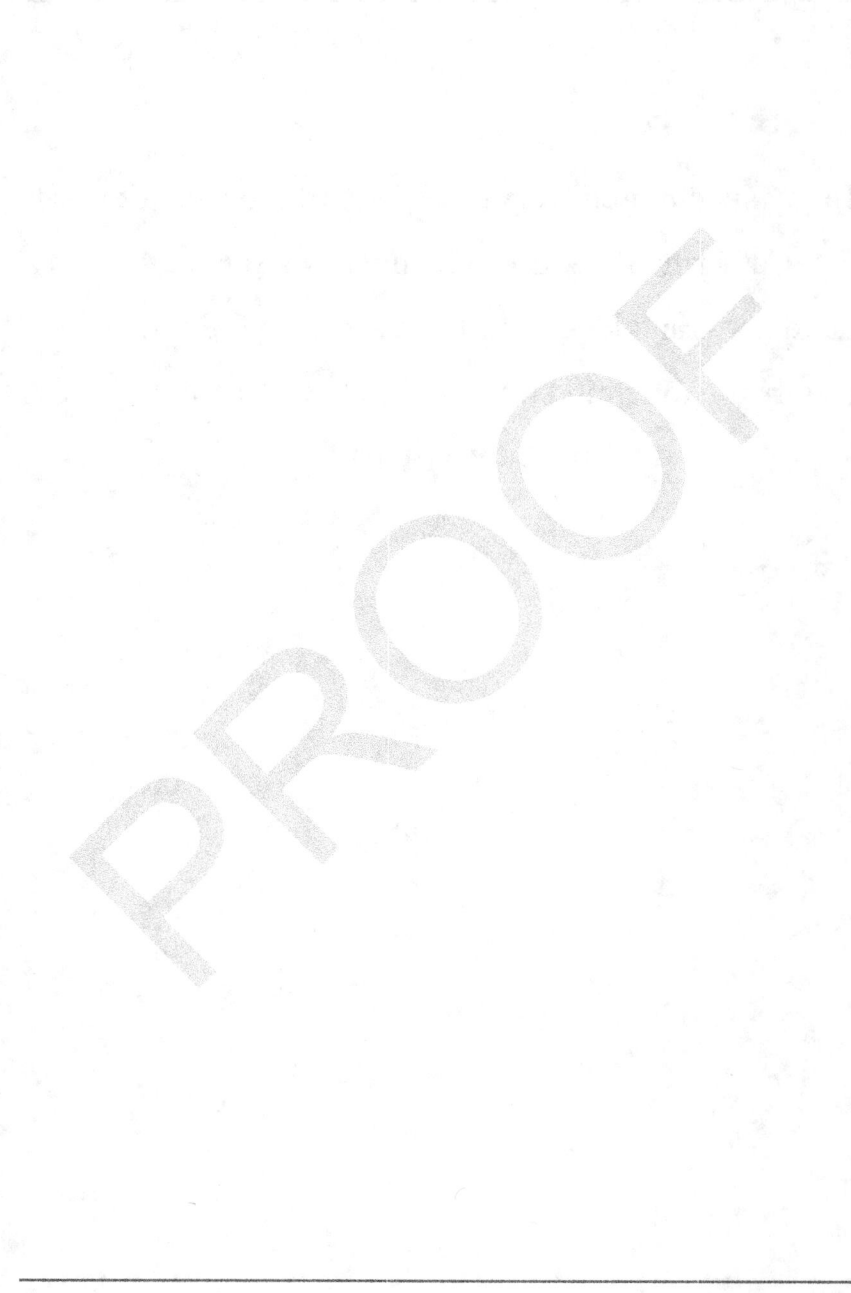

Special Thanks

Foundational Theology would not exist without the help of a lot of our staff and volunteers, including:

Mentors, Consultants, Teachers & Coaches

Chaplain Drake Austin
Randy Bissell
Commissioner Leo Blundo
Fr. Greg Boyle, S.J.
Rev. Bruno Mauricci
Charlene DeMoines
Mark Divine
Pastor Frank Esposito
Seth Godin
Pastor John Gundacker
Pastor Isiah Hill
Nancy Koehn, Ph.D.
Greg Marlow

Kathie McKenna
Lee McKenna
Rick Minch
Fr. Max Oliva, S.J.
Jeff Morgan
Mark Rowland
Dave Schmeck
Judge Richard Scotti, Esq.
Heather Stocker
Dennis Thornton
Chaplain Ralph Wade
Stephen Wesley
Dan Young

Partners & Supporters

Boxabl
Camino Verde Group
City Impact
Klamath Basin Behavioral Health
Nevada Outreach
No To Abuse
Nye Communities Coalition
Vegas Stronger
Veterans Administration

Contents

Acknowledgments

I would like to thank the inmates who attend "Bible Studies", the Corrections officers and Senior Staff in the Nye County jails for their help in producing this guide to foundational theology.

This would not have been possible without the students who, since 2011, almost incessantly make it clear that important, fundamental things were missing from their lives; plus, hundreds of hours spent with Dave and Randy from Prison Ministries of Texas; and weekly road trips with Chaplain Ralph (and Claudia) cumulatively, they helped me see and then walk the path needed to deliver this book. Proper respect goes to the Christian community in Pahrump; especially Pastor Frank Esposito (who started this ball rolling in 2021),

And two very special thanks: first, to our spiritual director, 50+ year Jesuit, Max Oliva, S.J. whose tempered encouragement of magis and, cautions of discernment, guides me daily, and second, to his anonymous donor who graciously helps provide for my personal needs.

AMDG

Disclaimer

I've learned from, reached out to, talked and debated with, studied-under, etc., the Mentors, Consultants, Teachers & Coaches identified above (and others) the following likely does not represent their beliefs or opinions. They are experts, (or are near-experts); whereas, I'm just a pilgrim, only trying to help those who are even less knowledgeable than me, start their Christian journey. Nothing herein is intended to be objectionable or controversial to any Christian beliefs.

In the event I've offended, mea culpa, mea culpa, mea culpa!

Preface

This book is the result of at least 50 years trying to understand the most basic questions related to God:

- Does God exist?
- If so, why so cryptic?
- Why are there so many Religions?
- Free will?
- The Trinity?
- Is there something after death?

I started life comfortably; raised in a successful family, well educated,[1] Roman Catholic, 6 great kids, etc. Later, during my darkest moments, in the hole in Chino State Prison, my heart was touched by St. Ignatius.

Since 2012, I have been living with and helping those who need help the most[2] learn the skills necessary to obtain stable, meaningful and livable wage employment. I've spent over 11,000 hours teaching in jails and prisons since 2011 and double that in the day-to-day, boots-on-the-ground, up-to-your-elbows in the

---

[1] 2nd generation Undergraduate degree from Santa Clara, the Jesuit University in Silicon Valley; Law School degree in San Diego

[2] Ex-felons, people with Substance Use Disorders, homeless, sex offenders, etc.

muck of human existence. It is hard, almost always showing that, "No good deed goes unpunished" [until it isn't].

Recently, I've been lucky enough to be able to go into the jails in Nye County and provide Spiritual guidance to inmates (i.e., "Bible Study") –Other than my Jesuit upbringing, I'm ill-equipped to discuss what God wants us to do as told through the prophets, his only son, Paul (formerly known as Saul) and the other New Testament authors.

I confess that I don't see much point of the Old Testament or the non-red letter parts of the New Testament. *Mea Culpa!*

What I learned though was that for most people, the nuances contained in the different versions of the Bible, and the almost countless explanations of what each Bible passage means (to the author, to God, to the Holy Spirit, to the reader, etc.) are not really that important when it comes to non-believers, pseudo-believers and believers with limited historical knowledge and/or context; they need a foundation upon which to build their Christian spirit (or perhaps, upon which the Holy Spirit may flow into them).

Hence, after decades of pondering, years of seeking answers, and months of addressing it face-to-face, this book was born.

And now, I will close, as Harvard Business School professor, Dr. Nancy Koehn, ends her emails to our students: "Onward".

Introduction

Lewis Carroll penned, *"If you don't know where you are going any road can take you there"*. Though many feel they know where they are going, (i.e., have a destination in mind); few are actually headed there (and it's virtually impossible to accidentally arrive anyway); and fewer know what it takes to actually get there. Unfortunately, most use outdated maps.

This book is not for "mature Christians"; it aims to answer some of the most-basic questions asked by **non-believers, pseudo-believers, and believers with limited historical knowledge and/or context**; namely,

- **Why should I commit?**
- **What's holding me back, and why?**

It is not a book on, or about, religion –that's best left to experts. Again, it's not for "mature" Christians –who will, no doubt, find it extremely lacking –perhaps completely "falling short of the mark". It is simply intended to assist three groups who are open to pursuing the Christian path: a) non-believers, b) pseudo-believers and c) believers with limited historical knowledge and/or context

This is an introduction to "foundational" (as distinct from "inspired" or "structured") theology[3]: What does it mean and why should you care? Right? (Admittedly, the title is almost "too clever by half"[4]).

Foundational Theology, as used herein, is what's underneath and supporting theology: a glimpse at Jesus' modus operandi. Think of it like how his words and deeds are the foundation of the New Testament (i.e., what the New Testament is built upon).

The goal is to help you better understand how and why pursuing the Christian path will result in a rewarding life of meaning and purpose. That's it, no big deal!

---

[3] **the·ol·o·gy** (noun) –the study of the nature of God and religious beliefs and theory when systematically developed.

[4] to be too confident of your own intelligence in a way that annoys other people

The Problem

<u>Confusion</u> for non-believers, pseudo-believers, and believers with limited historical knowledge and/or context

Should Religion require the use of an expert[5] trainer, guide, and/or teacher? Probably, but the most basic theology should be simple enough so that any reasonable person can master it without the need of an expert.

<u>Here's what causes confusion:</u>

- Why so many different Christian denominations?
- Why so many different Bibles?
- Why so many different Biblical interpretations?
- Why the need for pastors/teachers

These are all good questions and will, no doubt, be answered by the experts.

Our goal is simply to provide a foundation upon which the experts can build a strong faith.

Foundational theology must be easy to understand, easy to apply and relevant when it comes to learning about Christianity.

The Bible is a complex, God-inspired, collection of books. Quickly one learns that the more one learns the less they know (up

---

[5] **Clarke's 4th law** states that, *"For every expert there is an equal and opposite expert"*.

to a point) when studying the Bible.

Before diving into the description and application of Foundational Theology, let's have an overview of the landscape.

Further, we can't put the burden to solve the problem solely upon government and quasi-government agencies (i.e., the *status quo*); though they exist to provide resources for people in need, the human-economics are backwards.

- One resource provider (or a small team) especially those who work 8:00 to 5:00 M-F to many in-need people doesn't work.
- Many resources providers to one in-need person works.

Religion, Spirituality, Denominations ...

What is religion? Google's dictionary says: (noun)

"It's the belief in and worship of a superhuman power or powers, especially a God or gods.
  o   a particular <u>system of faith and worship</u>.
  o   a pursuit or interest to which someone ascribes supreme importance."

Here's a list of the major world religions (in billions), according to Wikipedia:

Christianity Roman Catholic Protestant	2.4 1.3 1.1	Abrahamic religions
Islam	**1.9**	Abrahamic religions
Hinduism	**1.2**	Indian religions
Buddhism	**0.5**	Indian religions
Folk religion	**0.4**	Regional

What is Spirituality? Google's dictionary says:

"The quality of being concerned with the human spirit or soul as opposed to material or physical things."

What is Christianity? Wikipedia explains it thus:

"It is an Abrahamic monotheistic religion based on the life and teachings of Jesus of Nazareth. It is the world's largest and most widespread religion with roughly 2.4 billion followers representing one-third of the global population. Its adherents, known as

Christians, are estimated to make up a majority of the population in 157 countries and territories. Most Christians believe that Jesus Christ is the Son of God, whose coming as the Messiah was prophesied in the Old Testament (the Hebrew Bible) and chronicled in the New Testament, published together as the Christian biblical canon.

Christianity remains culturally diverse in its Western and Eastern branches, as well as in its doctrines concerning justification and the nature of salvation, ecclesiology, ordination, and Christology. The creeds of various Christian denominations generally hold in common Jesus as the Son of God—the Logos incarnated—who ministered, suffered, and died on a cross, but rose from the dead for the salvation of humankind; and referred to as the gospel, meaning the "good news". Describing Jesus' life and teachings are the four canonical gospels of Matthew, Mark, Luke and John, with the Old Testament as the gospel's respected background."

Wikipedia reports that there are 200+ Protestant denominations.

What are Protestants? In the most simple form, they are the 1.1 billion "Non-Catholic Christians" who are members of the 200+ denominational and non-denominational churches formed in the past 500 years.

What are "Denominations"? Again, Wikipedia provides a good, simple answer:

"A Christian denomination is a distinct religious body within Christianity, identified by traits such as a name, organization and doctrine. Individual bodies, however, may use alternative terms to describe themselves, such as church, convention, communion, assembly, house, union, network, or sometimes fellowship. Divisions between one denomination and another are primarily defined by authority and doctrine. Issues regarding the **nature of Jesus, Trinitarianism, salvation, the authority of apostolic succession, eschatology, conciliarity, papal supremacy** and **papal primacy** among others may separate one denomination from another. Groups of denominations, often sharing broadly similar beliefs, practices, and historical ties—can be known as "branches of Christianity" or "denominational families" (e.g. Eastern or Western Christianity and their sub-branches). These "denominational families" are often imprecisely also called denominations."

What are "Non-Denominational" churches?

"Non-denominational" churches consist of churches which typically distance themselves from the confessionalism or creedalism of other Christian communities by not formally aligning with a specific Christian denomination. Many non-denominational churches have a congregationalist polity, which is self-governing without a higher church authority.

Nondenominational Christianity arose in the 18th century through the Restoration Movement, with followers organizing themselves simply as "Christians" and "Disciples of Christ".

The Solution

The solution enables non-believers, pseudo-believers, and believers with limited historical knowledge and/or context ("prospects") to feel that, with Jesus, they can join a community of kinship in order to navigate towards a life of meaning and purpose.

Prospects must

- see themselves as members of a community (not alone);
- feel that the community is non-judgmental;
- realize that community members truly want to "roll-up their sleeves" and help;
- learn to reciprocate by helping other members of the community;
- cultivate an orientation of learning, not having all the answers;
- leave the detrimental people, places and things from their past behind;
- demonstrate a commitment to change

What is Foundational Theology?

The sole aim of Foundational Theology is to introduce non-believers, pseudo- believers, and believers with limited historical knowledge and/or context ("prospects") to Jesus' words and deeds[6] through [tangible and intangible] <u>communities of kinship,</u> *before* learning Biblical doctrine regardless of whether it is from an expert. (NB, experts are essential, but confusion must be avoided at all costs).

Foundational Theology starts the process of helping prospects learn why they should act as Jesus taught (i.e., kinship); it sets the stage for Bible doctrine..

Communities of kinship reflect Jesus' teachings, and his way of being –especially as related to love and mercy (vs. sacrifice).

<u>Communities of kinship</u> are created by:

- replacing the belief that there is an "us" and a "them", with the belief that there is only "us";

- promoting the belief that, 'No kinship no justice; No kinship no equality; No kinship no peace.'; and

- <u>going to the margins</u> to dismantle the barriers that exclude.

<u>Going to the margins</u> occurs by:

- helping those whose burdens are more than they can bear,

---

[6] especially the "red-letter" parts of the Gospels (as opposed to the non-Gospel parts of the New Testament and the Old Testament).

- standing with the disposable so that the day will come when we stop throwing people away;

- standing with the demonized so that the demonizing will stop; and

- choosing to become different (i.e., not to make a difference) by experiencing what it's like to stand with the poor, the powerless, the voiceless, and those whose dignity has been denied;

What Foundational Theology is Not

- **No memorization:** It's not about interpreting the Bible or learning Bible doctrine –it's about building community in order to open the way for experts to teach Bible doctrine to those on fire for it.

- **No debates:** It's not complex or confusing –it's so simple that the only need for a Bible is to illustrate how Jesus' demonstrated kinship;

- **No divine intervention:** It's not about uncertain emotions –it's dependent upon reasoned compassion; and

- **No rules:** It's not about often complex formulas or "if - then" statements; it's about demonstrating justice, peace and equality

Memorization, apologetics, the Holy Spirit and structure are essential to a strong Christian belief –but only if and only if the solid foundation is properly set.

Why is the book Valuable?

A foundation built upon confusion is shaky indeed!

First, if the belief is that *solid lives are built on solid Christian principles*, doctrine[7] should follow, (i.e., not lead), basic Christian understanding.

Second, if the goal is to actually improve the lives of the living (as opposed to merely preparing for eternity), there must be practical things prospects can do;

Third, there must be systems of support (i.e., communities of kinship) because it is simply too hard (and frankly, unnecessary) to do it all on one's own.

Fourth, it's Maslow's Hierarchy[8]: people who are in "survival mode" mentality are not able to focus on much more than basic necessities (i.e., not self-actualization), so Biblical doctrine is often merely a dream, entertainment or per Marx "an opiate".

Fifth, Robert Frost was right, "Good fences make good neighbors"[9] (see Appendix)

---

[7] a belief or set of beliefs held and taught by a Church, political party, or other group.
[8] https://en.wikipedia.org/wiki/Maslow%27s_hierarchy_of_needs
[9] https://www.poetryfoundation.org/poems/44266/mending-wall

Why Now?

Because **crime, homelessness, drug and alcohol abuse, recidivism, and underemployment are increasing** (i.e., becoming a bigger, more expensive, problem) and will continue to do so into the foreseeable future. The costs of social programs are rising, yet producing less; everyone is blaming someone else. The bottomline: **The *status quo* is not working.**

New ideas and systems need to be advocated, supported and implemented before it's too late –expect a learning curve because there's no proven path.

Here's a new idea:

How about supporting "old ideas" that worked? (i.e., Reliance upon communities with strong values. Christian communities).

You can't do it alone!

Your Friends like you as you are

Additional Materials

Discussion Points

- Jesus went to the margins to be with those who needed it most; he did not focus on the most learned and wise;
- Jesus sought to build a communities of kinship;
  - Feeding the 5,000 was an example of kinship, (especially including the people sharing their meager possessions)
  - Healing the sick,
  - bread of life,
  - love;
- Kinship requires **peace** because you help your kin;
- Kinship requires **justice** because you treat your kin fairly
- Kinship requires **equality** because we are all loved equally by God

Foundational Theology Prayer[10]

This is not the place I've come to, it's the place I go from.

I go from here to help create a <u>community of kinship</u> such that it might be recognized as God's dream come true –no "us and them", just "us"-- because: No kinship no peace; No kinship no justice; No kinship no equality.

I imagine a circle of compassion and, I imagine nobody standing outside that circle; because my God does not share in the demonizing that we all engage in. And so,

I choose to go from here to help dismantle the barriers that exclude, –to stand at the margins because it's the only way they'll get erased.

I choose to stand with the poor, and the powerless, and the voiceless and with those whose dignity has been denied, –to stand with those whose burdens are more than they can bear.

I choose to join the exquisite mutual experience of knowing what it's like to stand with the easily despised and the readily left out, –to go from here to stand with the demonized so that the demonizing will stop;

I choose to stand with the disposable so that the day will come when we stop throwing people away.

I choose to go to the margins to make me different; not to change the people at the margins. No kinship no peace; No kinship no justice; No kinship no equality. Amen!

---

[10] Based on lectures from Greg Boyle, SJ (Homeboy Industries)

Foundational Theology in Action

- How can you start?
  - Spread the word;
-

Mending Wall
BY ROBERT FROST

Something there is that doesn't love a wall,
That sends the frozen-ground-swell under it,
And spills the upper boulders in the sun;
And makes gaps even two can pass abreast.
The work of hunters is another thing:
I have come after them and made repair
Where they have left not one stone on a stone,
But they would have the rabbit out of hiding,
To please the yelping dogs. The gaps I mean,
No one has seen them made or heard them made,
But at spring mending-time we find them there.
I let my neighbor know beyond the hill;
And on a day we meet to walk the line
And set the wall between us once again.
We keep the wall between us as we go.
To each the boulders that have fallen to each.
And some are loaves and some so nearly balls
We have to use a spell to make them balance:
'Stay where you are until our backs are turned!'
We wear our fingers rough with handling them.
Oh, just another kind of out-door game,
One on a side. It comes to little more:
There where it is we do not need the wall:
He is all pine and I am apple orchard.
My apple trees will never get across
And eat the cones under his pines, I tell him.
He only says, 'Good fences make good neighbors.'
Spring is the mischief in me, and I wonder
If I could put a notion in his head:
'Why do they make good neighbors? Isn't it
Where there are cows? But here there are no cows.

Before I built a wall I'd ask to know
What I was walling in or walling out,
And to whom I was like to give offense.
Something there is that doesn't love a wall,
That wants it down.' I could say 'Elves' to him,
But it's not elves exactly, and I'd rather
He said it for himself. I see him there
Bringing a stone grasped firmly by the top
In each hand, like an old-stone savage armed.
He moves in darkness as it seems to me,
Not of woods only and the shade of trees.
He will not go behind his father's saying,
And he likes having thought of it so well
He says again, 'Good fences make good neighbors.'

Notes

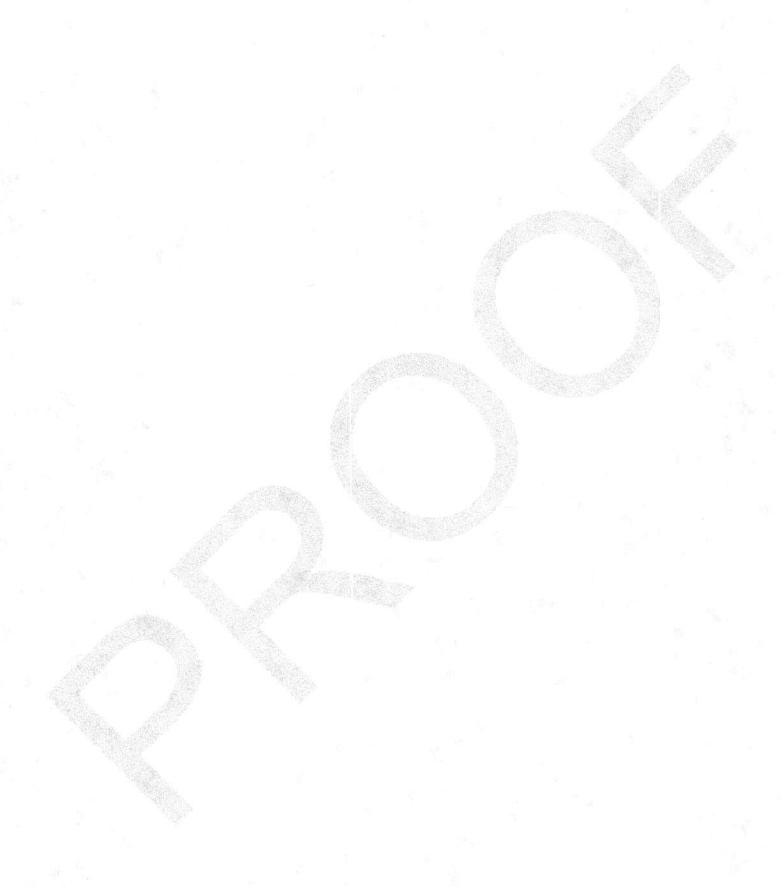